J940·55

4/9?

msc .

AFTERMATH OF WAR

ROBIN CROSS

Wayland

AFTERMATH OF WAR

Other titles:

Children's War
Cities at War
Propaganda
Technology of War
Victims of War
Women and War
World Leaders

Cover illustration: 'All Marxist roads lead to Moscow!' A 1953 German Christian Democrat poster warns that left-wing sympathies will lead to Soviet domination.
Contents page: A Christian Democrat (CDU) election poster featuring the Soviet leader Krushchev demanding 'Bring down Adenauer'. Adenauer, the CDU leader, was a fierce opponent of communism.

First published in 1994 by
Wayland (Publishers) Ltd
61 Western Rd, Hove
East Sussex BN3 1JD, England

© Copyright 1994 Wayland (Publishers) Ltd

Series editor: Paul Mason
Designer: Mark Whitchurch

British Library Cataloguing in Publication Data
    Cross, Robin
    Technology of War-(Era of the Second World
    War Series)
    I.Title II.Series
    940.55

ISBN 0-7502-1161-X

Typeset by Mark Whitchurch
Printed and bound in Italy by Rotolito Lombarda
S.p.A.

Illustration acknowledgements
Thanks to John Yates for providing the artwork. We would also like to thank the following for allowing their photos to be reproduced in this title: Archiv fur Kunst und Geschichte, Berlin/Image Select cover, 3, 24; Camera Press 6, 33, 35, 40, 41, 44; Eye Ubiquitous 9; Imperial War Museum 5; Popperfoto 4, 5 top, 7, 10, 12, 14 both, 16, 21, 22, 23, 29, 37 bottom, 39 both, 42, 43; Topham 8, 13, 15, 17, 19, 20 both, 25, 26, 27, 28, 30, 32, 34, 36, 37 top, 38.

But within three years Krupp had been released and was back at the head of Germany's biggest steel business.

Krupp's release highlighted the difficulties of Denazification. After the war the US, Britain and France tried 170,000 individuals for their wartime activities, but many received only token punishment. At its height in Germany the Nazi Party had eight million members. They could not all be punished. In some professions membership of the Nazi Party was essential for success.

The German lawyers who defended those on trial at Nuremberg had all been Nazi Party members. Many of the businessmen, technicians and teachers needed to restore Germany to economic health and political stability had been Party members. Most of them claimed to have shed their Nazi beliefs. Some, at least, were sincere. By 1949 Britain and the USA had decided to let sleeping dogs lie: their priority was the fight against communism. But outside Germany there was much unease that people with Nazi connections were allowed to occupy important positions in public and business life so soon after the downfall of the Third Reich.

A pre-war Nazi Party rally near the town of Nuremberg. The fact that eight million Germans had been Nazi Party members made it difficult for the Allied victors to decide who should be held responsible in the years following the war.

Marshal Philippe Pétain, head of France's Vichy government, during his trial for treason in 1945. His death sentence was commuted to life imprisonment. Pétain died in 1951. His deputy, Pierre Laval, who had worked more closely with the Germans, was executed at the end of the war.

In the meantime a number of major war criminals slipped through the net. With good luck and the right connections a wanted Nazi could obtain a false International Red Cross passport and an entry visa to a foreign country. From 1947 senior Nazis on the run were able to use escape routes - often to South America - established by ODESSA, an organization run by former members of the SS which posed as a charity. As many as 20,000 wanted Nazis escaped this way. Among them was Adolf Eichmann, the chief Gestapo official responsible for carrying out the Final Solution (see box on opposite page).

Sometimes Nazis were helped to escape by their former enemies. Klaus Barbie, the Butcher of Lyons, had been responsible for the torture and execution of many captured members of the French Resistance. After the war Barbie fell into the hands of the US forces, who used him to identify French communists who had fought with the Resistance. The USA blocked all efforts to extradite Barbie to France and in 1950 assisted his flight to Bolivia. It was not until 1983 that the French were able to obtain Barbie's return from Bolivia. He was found guilty of crimes against humanity and in 1987 sentenced to life imprisonment.

The hunt for war criminals continues. But the passing of the years makes it increasingly difficult to gather the evidence and witnesses against those accused of committing war crimes as long as 50 years ago. The trial in Germany of personnel who ran the extermination camps at Maidanek began in 1975 and lasted until 1983. In the summer of 1993, 67 people living in Britain were being investigated in connection with war crimes committed during the Second World War.

Adolf Eichmann

During the war Adolf Eichmann had been responsible for the deaths of millions. He was the SS officer in charge of controlling the Jewish population of the German-occupied territories. In 1942 he was put in charge of the Final Solution of the 'Jewish problem'. He proceeded to organize the death camps, and the transport of the Jews to them, with great efficiency. He vanished in 1945, but was discovered in Brazil in 1960, living under the name of Ricardo Clement. He was kidnapped by an Israeli group and placed on trial in Tel Aviv, where he was sentenced to death and hanged in 1962. To the end, Eichmann appeared to have no hatred of the Jews but merely saw his task as fulfilling the wishes of the German leader, Adolf Hitler.

Adolf Eichmann is found guilty of crimes against humanity at the end of his trial in Israel in 1961. Throughout the trial he sat in a bullet-proof box, to protect him from would-be assassins.

Many Jews, in particular, have never forgotten or forgiven their persecutors. Simon Wiesenthal, an Austrian Jew and survivor of the death camps, has devoted his life to tracking down some 1,200 Nazi war criminals from his Jewish Documentation Centre in Vienna.

Hand in hand with Denazification went the punishment of collaborators - those who had actively helped the Germans in the countries Germany had occupied. When these countries were liberated by the Allies, the collaborators faced the wrath of their fellow citizens.

In France the purge of collaborators - known as the purification - lasted from September 1944 to the end of 1949. According to the official figures, there were 175,000 cases, resulting in 120,000 sentences. Of these, 4,785 were death sentences, of which nearly 2,000 were carried out. The aged Marshal Pétain, head of the collaborationist Vichy government, was sentenced to death, but this was commuted to life imprisonment. His deputy, Pierre Laval, was executed on 15 October 1945.

Members of the French Resistance step in to protect a trouserless suspected collaborator from the anger of Parisians, after the liberation of the French capital in August 1944.

With their backs to the camera, two Belgian women in the tiger cage of Antwerp zoo await trial for collaboration. Different countries dealt with collaborators with different harshnesses: in Belgium collaborators were dealt with severely.

After the liberation of France the Resistance settled many old scores on the spot. It has been estimated that they executed up to 50,000 collaborators without trial. Woman who had slept with German soldiers had their heads shaved and were paraded through the streets.

There had been relatively few active members of the French Resistance during the war. The overwhelming majority of people passively accepted the German occupation. When France was liberated in the summer of 1944 many thousands falsely claimed to have been members of the Resistance all along. Collaborators who were brought to trial immediately after liberation were scapegoats for the collective guilt felt by the French for the wartime occupation of their country. As a result they often received far harsher sentences than those who faced trial later.

To this day the French have found it extremely difficult to come to terms with the shame of defeat and occupation in 1940. One of the reactions has been to try to sweep things under the carpet. Several important French politicians of the post-war years had pasts tainted by collaboration with the Germans, but this was not allowed to affect their political careers.

The severity of the purge of collaborators and war criminals varied. In Austria, where the roots of Nazism ran deep, only 9,000 stood trial and there were just 35 death sentences. In contrast, after the liberation of Belgium 634,000 cases were opened, a huge figure for a population of eight million. Eventually nearly 90,000 people were brought to trial. About 77,000 received sentences. More than 4,000 death sentences were passed, but of these only 230 were carried out. In Denmark, where there had been no death penalty even during the German

occupation, 46 collaborators were executed out of 112 sentenced to death. In Norway collaborators were pursued with particular thoroughness: 633 out of every 100,000 citizens were punished, compared to 93 out of 100,000 in France. The leader of the Norwegian Nazi Party, Vidkun Quisling, whose name became an international slang word for traitor, was sentenced to death and executed in Oslo on 24 October 1945.

In the Netherlands a system of out-of-court settlements was devised to deal with the huge backlog of collaborators waiting trial in the autumn of 1945. If the accused did not agree to the proposed settlement - a fine in the case of lesser offenders - he or she would stand trial. Not surprisingly, perhaps, over 80 per cent agreed to settle.

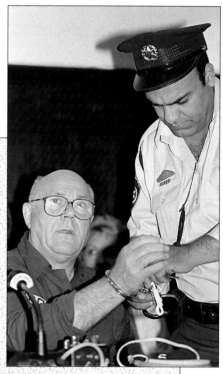

May 14 1990: an Israeli policeman removes John Demjanjuk's handcuffs during his appeal against a conviction for war crimes.

John Demjanjuk

The problem of identifying war criminals after the passing of 50 years was highlighted by the case of John Demjanjuk, a Ukrainian who had emigrated to the USA in the early 1960s. In 1981 the US Justice Department stripped him of his US citizenship because he had concealed his wartime membership of the SS. In the course of the investigations Demjanjuk was identified as Ivan the Terrible, a guard in the extermination camp at Treblinka, where up to one million Jews were killed between July 1942 and September 1943. Ivan the Terrible had tortured and mutilated his victims on their way to the gas chambers and murdered others with his own hands. Demjanjuk was extradited to Israel in February 1986. At his trial he was identified as Ivan the Terrible by five survivors of Treblinka and sentenced to death. The case against Demjanjuk fell apart when he appealed against the death sentence. After the collapse of the USSR his lawyers obtained fresh documents from the archives of the Soviet security service. These showed that Ivan was another man called Ivan Marchenko. Demjanjuk, who had consistently lied about his wartime activities, had been a camp guard, but at Sobibor not Treblinka. There was no record of what he had done at Sobibor. On 29 July 1993 Demjanjuk was freed. Very quickly the Israeli courts agreed to hear a petition that he should be tried for war crimes at Sobibor, but this failed for lack of evidence.

In the court

THERE HE IS! screamed one of the witnesses, Pinhas Epstein, red with rage. Demjanjuk listened impassively to his headphones, hearing a Ukranian translation of stories of live babies being thrown into burial pits and inmates being forced to pull gold teeth from corpses on their way to cremation.

Divided Germany

In February 1945, three months before the end of the war in Europe, Roosevelt, Stalin and Churchill met at Yalta in the Crimea. One of the most important topics for discussion at Yalta was the post-war division of Germany.

The Allies were agreed on the need to ensure that Germany did not produce a Fourth Reich and spark off a new world war. The Soviets and the French had been invaded twice by Germany in the previous fifty years. They were determined that Germany would never again be a threat to their security. Several different schemes had been hatched to prevent Germany from rising again. General de Gaulle, head of the provisional French government, had proposed that Germany be split into a large number of small, independent states. This coincided with a US plan, devised by Henry Morgenthau, the US Treasury Secretary. At the Quebec conference in September 1944 he submitted a plan under which post-war Germany would be stripped of its industry and converted to an entirely agricultural economy. The plan was at first supported by Roosevelt and Churchill, but it never became official policy because it was realized that it was impractical. When the Germans had got wind of the plan, Josef Goebbels, Hitler's Minister of Propaganda, had made much of the fact that Morgenthau was a Jew and his plan provided ample warning of what would happen to Germany if it lost the war. Meanwhile the British had been working on a plan - codenamed Rankin C - for the division of

East meets West: American and Soviet soldiers shake hands at the German town of Torgau on the Elbe on 25 April 1945. The end of the war in Europe was only a week away. The friendliness between the two countries did not survive for long.

Germany between themselves, the USA and the USSR, with a joint occupation of Berlin, the German capital. At Yalta the Big Three agreed to the Rankin C plan, with the addition of a smaller French zone in the Saarland, carved out of the British and US zones of occupation. The zoning arrangements agreed at Yalta were confirmed at the Potsdam conference held in the southern suburbs of Berlin in July 1945.

For Germans in the months following the end of the war there was little time to reflect on the past or worry about the future. They had to concentrate on survival. One in every five inhabitants of the western zones was a refugee, known as a 'displaced person' or DP. Thousands of them roamed the countryside in lawless bands. In the British sector of Berlin about 20,000 refugees were arriving every day both from Russian-occupied Germany and the large slice of pre-war Germany given to Poland at Potsdam. Food was running short. In 1946 the authorities in the British and US zones cut the food rations to 900

Anything to declare? German police search a Berliner's shopping bag for black market items in August 1945. Rations in the British zone of Berlin were less than some concentration camp inmates had been given, so Berliners had little choice but to trade on the black market, even though it was illegal.

The Black Market

At the end of the war Germany was in ruins. Economic life had come to a halt. In the cities people searched the rubble for anything they could use or sell. The occupying Allies introduced strict controls over the supply of money. This encouraged the growth of a hidden economy - the black market - which became the chief means of survival for the occupied and a source of profit for the occupiers. Cigarettes replaced money as the units of exchange. With enough cigarettes you could buy anything. For 25 cartons of cigarettes a US soldier could buy a Leica camera and sell it in the USA for $600. With $600 he could buy 750 cartons of cigarettes and trade himself towards a small fortune. Among Germans a new profession was invented: the *Kippensammler*, a collector of cigarette ends. With seven cigarette ends you could make a single cigarette and enter a world of barter in which an expensive Persian rug might be exchanged for a sack of potatoes. The black market kept thousands of people on the move, travelling on packed trains in search of scarce items for exchange.

calories a day - near starvation level. Women queued outside the barracks occupied by Allied troops to collect their leftovers. Few hospitals had been left standing when the fighting ended and medical supplies were scarce. Typhoid and dysentery spread rapidly.

Germany's cities had been flattened by Allied bombers. In Dusseldorf nine out of every ten houses were uninhabitable. There were no recognizable streets in the centre of Berlin, just endless piles of rubble. As winter approached the situation grew worse. The coal mines in the Ruhr were producing only 25,000 tonnes a day, compared with 400,000 tonnes a day before the war. The canal and rail networks that were needed to transport food and fuel to where they were needed most had been wrecked by the fighting at the end of the war.

In the middle of this gloom and despair there was a ray of hope. Although German industrial production had come to a standstill, much of the heavy equipment in Germany's factories remained undamaged under the debris. In the Ruhr only about 20 per cent of the heavily bombed factories were beyond repair. Here, under shattered roofs and piles of twisted metal, lay the seeds of the spectacular German economic recovery of the 1950s.

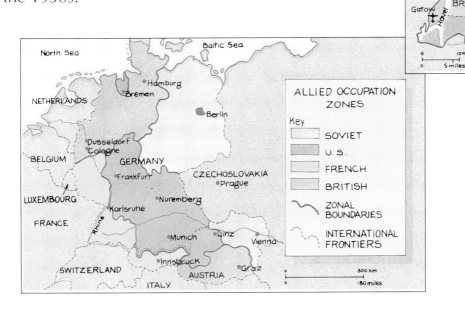

Contrasts in power: Britain and the USA

The USA and Britain emerged from the war as victorious allies but not equal partners. The USA was now the richest and most powerful nation in the world, and the sole possessor of the atomic bomb. While its economic rivals were tearing each other to pieces the USA had remained physically untouched by war. In five years the US economy had leapt ahead. Industry had expanded by 40 per cent and the United States' Gross National Product had risen by 60 per cent. The war had brought unparalleled prosperity to millions of Americans. Between 1940 and 1945 the farmers' net cash income more than quadrupled; the weekly wages of industrial workers rose by 70 per cent.

A sleek Pontiac saloon, symbol of the US post-war affluence, the foundations of which were laid during the Second World War. While Europe was ruined, America was physically untouched by the war, and its industry expanded greatly during the war years.

In theory Britain remained one of the most powerful nations on earth. At Yalta in February 1945 Churchill had sat alongside the Soviet leader Stalin and the US President Roosevelt at the conference which decided the shape of post-war Europe. Britain was one of the Big Three. Unlike her European neighbours, Britain had not suffered the horrors of Nazi occupation. Her towns and factories had been badly knocked about by German bombs and rockets, but the fighting across Europe had caused much greater damage.

In Britain wartime hardships continued long after 1945. A poster in this café reminds diners not to 'ask for bread unless you really want it.' In Britain bread rationing was introduced only after the war.

On VE-Day, 8 May 1945, the British celebrated victory in Europe. Bonfires were lit all over Britain, their flames stirring memories of the fires that had raged during the Blitz in the winter of 1940-41. The mood of celebration did not last long. In reality Britain was almost bankrupt. The economist John Maynard Keynes considered that the nation was facing a 'financial Dunkirk'.

The price of victory had bitten deeply into Britain's wealth. To pay for the war, Britain had sold £4 billion of overseas investments. Her industries were badly run down. The coal mines, on which virtually all heavy industry depended, were in particularly poor shape. On 23 August 1945, eight days after the end of the war in the Far East, the USA abruptly cancelled the Lend-Lease agreement by which it had fed and armed the British since 1941. Now the British would have to pay for US imports from their dwindling reserves of dollars.

In contrast to the photo above, this US diner is well-stocked with coffee and doughnuts, and seems a warmer, more comfortable place.

The USA was no longer Britain's grocer and armourer, but was forced to step in as its banker. In the winter of 1946, after weeks of extremely tough negotiations, the British were saved from bankruptcy by a US loan of $4.5 billion.

The loan ensured economic survival but did not bring an end to the deprivations the British had suffered during the war. Food rationing not only remained in force but became more severe. In July 1946 bread was rationed - a measure never imposed during the war but introduced in order to feed people in the British-occupied zone of Germany. Clothes continued to be rationed until 1949, petrol until 1950 and some categories of food, for example sweets, until 1954.

In the middle of these economic difficulties Britain's newly elected Labour government was embarking on an ambitious programme of social and industrial reform. The end of the war in Europe had also seen the end of Britain's wartime coalition government. In the general election of July 1945 the Labour Pary won a landslide victory over the Conservatives, whose leader, Winston Churchill, had been Britain's Prime Minister since May 1940. The Conservatives had expected Churchill's popularity to carry his party to victory. In Britain he had been the dominating figure of the war. But the British people decided that Churchill's qualities as a war leader were not suited to the different demands of peace.

A long queue waits for scarce supplies of potatoes in north London in the summer of 1947. A policeman makes sure that order is maintained. For the British peace brought harsher rationing measures than the war.

Unemployed workers clash with police in London's East End in 1930. In 1945 the British looked forward to a world in which there would be no unemployment and scenes like this would not be repeated. A Labour government was voted into power.

In the middle years of the war the thoughts of British soldiers and civilians had turned to the future. They were determined that when peace came it would be accompanied by social change. There would be no return to the dole queues of the 1930s. The coalition government recognized these aspirations. In December 1942 it produced the Beveridge Report, which proposed a national scheme of social insurance 'from cradle to grave'.

Sir William Beveridge's proposals to attack the '*five giants of Want, Disease, Ignorance, Squalor and Idleness*' expressed in the clearest terms the overwhelming public desire that the social improvements and fair shares of wartime would be carried over into the peace. The shared hardships of war had temporarily broken down many of the old social divisions of class and income, and had heightened expectations of post-war change.

In the public mind, however, the Conservative Party was associated with unemployment of the 1930s and the disasters of the early years of the war. In contrast the Labour members of the wartime coalition could take much of the credit for the success of domestic wartime planning and the improvements in social services that accompanied them. The proposals for a post-war welfare state would not be safe in Conservative hands. Labour's commitment to reform won them nearly 12 million votes against 10 million for the Conservatives.

Within 12 months the Labour government had launched a programme of social reform and the nationalization of industry. Eventually coal, the railways and public transport, electricity, gas and the steel industry were taken into public ownership. The National Insurance Act provided the whole adult population with sickness, unemployment and retirement benefits. In 1948 the National Health Service was introduced, providing free medical treatment for all. Such was its popularity that it was soon the second highest item of government expenditure.

The Labour government's attempt to build a new Britain began to falter in the harsh winter of 1946-7, when deep snow blanketed the country and brought industry to a virtual halt. Housing, too, remained a problem the government was unable to solve. Its target was the completion of 400,000 new houses a year. But in 1948 only 230,000 houses were built, compared with the 350,000 built in 1938, when the British economy was still suffering from the effects of the economic slump of the early 1930s.

The big freeze

The British winter of 1946-7 was the coldest for 53 years. Sixteen degrees of frost - unremarkable in Siberia or Saskatchewan but virtually unknown in Britain - brought the country to a standstill. Icebergs were seen off the east coast. In Lancashire a farmer borrowed a pneumatic drill to dig up his parsnips. Coal supplies ran out, which was a severe blow to the public's confidence in the Labour government's nationalization programme. Factories ground to a halt. At home people shivered without heat or light. Unemployment soared to 2.5 million and exports fell away to nothing. In the middle of March 1947 three months of ice and four-metre snowdrifts gave way to a thaw. There was heavy flooding in which crops were ruined and thousands of cattle and sheep drowned. After all this, in the summer of 1947 there was a prolonged drought.

A frozen-up double-decker bus in February 1947.

Britain's continuing economic weakness meant that the government could no longer afford to meet all its international commitments. The days of imperial power were just a memory. In July 1947 the British Foreign Secretary, Ernest Bevin, told the USA that Britain could no longer provide military and economic aid to Greece and Turkey, which had been a British responsibility since the end of the war. The Americans stepped in. President Truman asked the US Congress for a $4 billion aid package. He declared, *'The free peoples of the world must turn to us for support.'* It was support on a scale that only the USA could provide. The US President's offer of aid to nations resisting either direct or indirect communist aggression became known as the Truman Doctrine.

By 1950 Britain's Labour government had run out of steam. A vast programme of rearmament, caused by the outbreak of the Korean War, increased the demand for scarce resources. To try to solve part of its problems, the government introduced charges for some of the services provided by the National Health. This caused a huge row within the Labour Party followed by electoral defeat by the Conservatives in 1951. Much of the Labour legacy remained in the following years. There was a general agreement on the aims of British governments - full employment, rising living standards and an expanding welfare state - which was not questioned until the arrival in power of Margaret Thatcher in 1979.

The Chinese Communist leader, Mao Tse-tung, pictured with one of his army commanders during China's war with invading Japanese forces (1937-45). Although they were on the same side during the war, when it ended the Chinese became an opponent of the USA in Southeast Asia. To stop the spread of communism, US President Truman offered financial support to non-communist countries all round the world.

Rebuilding Western Europe

In August 1914, on the eve of the First World War, the nations of Western Europe dominated the economic and political maps of the world. London, Paris and Berlin were the great financial centres, where over 80 per cent of the world's investments were made. European states had the strongest armies and controlled vast tracts of Africa and Asia. Optimism in Europe ran high, but the next 30 years were to bring about a profound change in the global balance of power.

By 1914 the USA had overtaken Britain and Germany as the world's leading industrial power. It emerged from the First World War even stronger as its European rivals tore each other to pieces. Even though the USA followed a policy of isolationism until 1939 its economy remained the most important in the world.

In the Second World War, which the USA entered in December 1941, the United States was one of the two major contributors to the defeat of Germany. The other was the USSR. In May 1945, with Hitler dead and the Third Reich in ruins, these two great non-European military powers were established in the heart of Europe and were to decide the future political and economic shape of the continent.

At the end of the war Europe's self-inflicted wounds were savage. Even in 1947, two years after the end of the war, Winston Churchill wrote: 'What is Europe? A rubbish heap, a charnel-house, a breeding ground of pestilence and hate.'

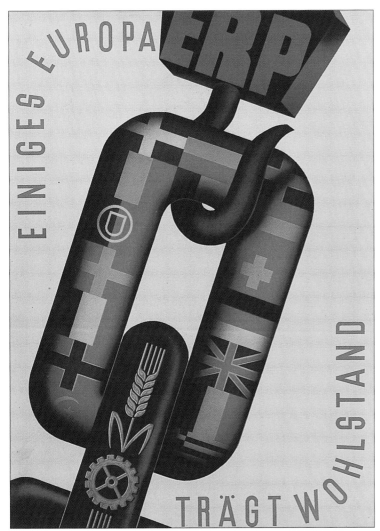

EINIGES EUROPA

ERP

TRÄGT WOHLSTAND

A German poster shows the European Recovery Programme (ERP), more popularly known as the Marshall Plan, hauling the countries of Europe towards economic recovery.

The road from rubbish heap to recovery was closely bound up with the economic power of the USA. Allied victory had been secured by US industrial and technological might, but the USA had driven a hard bargain to ensure that its economic supremacy continued after the war.

To meet their wartime bills, the British were forced to sell off many of their overseas assets, particularly in Latin America. Big US corporations like General Motors and Standard Oil moved in to fill the gap left by the British.

American big business had no intention of giving up its advantages at the end of the war. In July 1944 representatives of 44 nations met at Bretton Woods, in the American state of New Hampshire, to discuss a new international monetary system. The conference, which was dominated by the USA, set up the International Monetary Fund (IMF) and, later, the World Bank, both of which were financed by the United States. National currencies were tied to the US dollar, and the US Federal Reserve became the world's central bank, an arrangement that was to last until 1971. The Americans also gained reluctant acceptance of an 'open door' policy, which guaranteed the USA unhindered access to overseas markets. The overwhelming feeling among US business and political leaders was that what was good for American business was good for the world.

As the war drew to a close, traditional US isolationism began to reassert itself. In the summer of 1945 the United States' immediate aim was the speediest possible withdrawal from Europe. However, the countries of Western Europe remained financially dependent on the USA. As the months went by they showed little sign of struggling back on to their feet. By 1947 they owed the IMF and the World Bank $5.5 billion. Unable to compete economically with the United States, they were in the grip of a 'dollar shortage'. Economic crisis brought political problems in its wake. The British were cutting back their commitments in Greece, where the government was fighting a guerilla war against communist groups supported by Albania, Yugoslavia and Bulgaria. There was unrest in Italy, where there were over 2.5 million unemployed and soaring inflation. The communist parties in both Italy and France organized a series of damaging strikes aimed at bringing down the weak coalition governments in their countries. Economic collapse in Western Europe would leave a political vacuum that could be filled by the USSR.

Above all, it was the communist threat that prompted the USA to step in. In a speech to a graduating class at Harvard University on 5 June 1947 the US Secretary of State, General George Marshall, offered aid to all the countries of Europe on the condition that they co-operated to produce a plan for recovery.

Within hours the British Foreign Secretary, Ernest Bevin, seized on Marshall's signal as a firm offer. Acting on his own initiative, he cabled acceptance. He later told a group of American journalists that Marshall's speech was like *a lifeline to sinking men*. For the British there was a conflict between pride and poverty. Poverty won. Britain was no longer a global superpower: the USA now was. Without US aid the British government would have been forced to bring in even harsher rationing measures.

General George Marshall, the USA's wartime Army Chief of Staff and, from 1947-9, US Secretary of State. In June 1947 Marshall proposed that the USA should help rebuild the world economy to enable free institutions to flourish after the ravages of war.

The idea floated by Marshall was quickly fleshed out as the European Recovery Plan, but was popularly known as Marshall Aid. It was offered to all European countries, including the USSR and its Eastern European satellite states. The Soviet leader, Josef Stalin, was not prepared to join a programme to revive the capitalist economies of Western Europe. On 2 July the Soviet Foreign Minister, Vlachislav Molotov, walked out of the Paris conference on the Recovery Plan, dragging the reluctant Eastern European states behind him. This exit at Paris confirmed the division of Europe into two hostile camps. The Soviets were blamed for refusing an offer of apparent generosity by the USA.

Over the next five years 16 of Europe's non-communist countries received $13 billion worth of aid. It had a number of important effects. First, it helped economies that had begun to recover. Marshall Aid enabled them to go on a spending spree, financing major reconstruction programmes which turned into a general economic boom in the 1950s. Raw materials, fuel and heavy equipment poured into Europe, boosting transport, agriculture and industry, the building blocks of economic recovery. By the autumn of 1950, European industrial output was running 35 per cent above the pre-war level. Steel production had increased by 70 per cent, that of motor vehicles by 150 per cent and refined oil products by 200 per cent. Italy and West Germany (which had come into being in September 1949) lagged behind, but their economies had been more seriously affected by the war. Europe as a whole was well on the way to a recovery that was only briefly interrupted by the outbreak of the Korean War in 1950.

Italian communists on the march in Rome in July 1948 after the attempted assassination of their leader Palmiero Togliatti. In 1948 the Italian communist party, with 2 million members, was the strongest outside the communist bloc. Countries with communists in the government were encouraged by the USA to sack them: when Italy's prime minister sacked his communist colleagues in 1947, the USA responded with a $600 million aid package.

With improved economic health came political stability. The Recovery Plan also pointed the way to increased economic co-operation and integration. The planning of the reconstruction schemes paid for by Marshall Aid was handled by the Organization for European Economic Co-operation (OEEC) in January 1958.

A French communist demonstration at Vincennes, near Paris. In 1946 the French communist party numbered nearly a million. In post-war years it could count on the consistent support of about 25 per cent of French voters. Nevertheless, in May 1947 France's communists were removed from the government: the USA immediately granted France $200 million in aid.

Winston Churchill called Marshall Aid *'one of the most unsordid acts in the history of a nation.'* In reality Marshall Aid was motivated by more down-to-earth US economic and political interests. A poverty-stricken Europe was a Europe in which US-made goods could not be sold.

Marshall Aid also proved a powerful weapon in the Cold War against communism. Financial help from the USA came with political strings attached. Governments with communist ministers found they could not get US aid. Above all, Marshall Aid ensured that West Germany, in the front line of the Cold War, was securely locked within the framework of a general economic recovery in Western Europe.

In January 1949 the USSR responded to Marshall Aid by setting up the Council for Mutual Economic Assistance (COMECON). The aim of the Soviet-controlled organization was an improvement in trade between the USSR and other East European states. Its original members were Albania, Bulgaria, Czecho-slovakia, Hungary, Poland, Romania and the USSR.

The Cold War

Red Army units that took part in the battle for Berlin parade outside the ruined Reichstag building in May 1945. Hitler had wanted to destroy communism, but in the end the war his armies had begun brought a communist occupation of Berlin.

In August 1945 the Allies achieved total victory over Germany and Japan. But the unity of the wartime alliance did not survive the end of the war. World War was replaced by Cold War, a long period of tension and conflict between East and West, from which we are only just emerging.

Historians continue to argue about the origins of the Cold War in Europe. Its principal cause was quite simple: Adolf Hitler's invasion of the Soviet Union in June 1941. One of Hitler's aims had been to destroy communism, but the result was to embed communism in the heart of Europe. After suffering a series of shattering defeats, the USSR gained the upper hand and drove the Germans westward. When the war ended the Red Army was 160 km from the River Rhine, occupying the whole of Eastern Europe and most of the Balkans. Although the USSR had suffered huge losses during the war, and the majority of its cities and factories west of the Urals lay in ruins, it was now the strongest military power in Europe. At the same time, the Soviet leaders were painfully aware that the USA had the atomic bomb, while they did not.

The future of post-war Europe had been discussed at two wartime conferences, Tehran (1943) and Yalta (1944), attended by Roosevelt, Churchill and Stalin. By the time the Big Three met at Yalta in February 1945, the cracks in the wartime alliance were opening up. Churchill was deeply suspicious about Stalin's ambitions in Europe. Roosevelt, on the other hand, was convinced that he could 'do business' with the Soviet

leader. He was also eager to secure the USSR's speedy entry into the war against Japan, which was occupying Manchuria, part of China.

Roosevelt was prepared to make important concessions to Stalin over Eastern Europe, which was firmly under the control of the Red Army. Together they formed a united front against Churchill, who wanted to map out the shape of post-war Europe in detail. Instead, the US produced a Declaration on Liberated Europe. This provided for the right of all peoples to choose the form of government under which they wished to live.

This meant nothing to Stalin. Above all, he was determined that after the war Poland - the age-old invasion route into Russia - would remain under Soviet control. Beyond the boundaries of an enlarged Soviet Union would stretch a protective buffer of satellite Eastern European nations which the Soviet Union had either liberated (Poland and Czechoslovakia) or invaded (Hungary, Romania, Bulgaria). Stalin had a simple and brutal approach to these matters. He declared, *'Everyone imposes his own system as far as his army can reach. It cannot be otherwise.'*

In return for Stalin's promise to enter the war against Japan, Roosevelt was prepared to let the Soviets have their way over Poland. In September 1939 the British had gone to war over Poland. In 1945 they were in no position to guarantee the Poles an independent and democratic future. Poland was to be 'a friend of the Soviet Union'.

The sole reason for the wartime alliance was the defeat of Nazi Germany. Once Germany had surrendered that reason disappeared. When the Big Three met for the last time at Potsdam in July-August 1945, the cracks in the wartime alliance had become a yawning gulf.

Churchill realized that Stalin had created a Soviet empire. In a speech he made at Fulton, Missouri, on 5 March 1946, Churchill warned: *'From Stettin in the Baltic to Trieste in the Adriatic, an iron curtain has descended across the continent* (of Europe). *Behind that line lie the capitals of the ancient states of Central and Eastern Europe.'* At the time this speech did not go down too well with the US government, which was still pursuing a policy of moderation and concessions with the Soviet Union.

In Eastern Europe Stalin moved step by step. There was not one satellite state where the communists were in a majority. They were not popular. One by one the non-communist members of the coalition governments formed after liberation were removed. The tactics used varied: bogus treason charges, faked fascist plots, sometimes outright terror. Eventually in Bulgaria, Romania, Poland, Hungary and Czechoslovakia the coalition governments were replaced by Popular Fronts in which communists held all the important jobs. Then the Popular Fronts were replaced by one-party communist régimes.

There was one important exception to this process. In Yugoslavia, Marshal Tito's communist-led partisans had liberated the country with little outside help and had set up a communist government. The Yugoslavs

Winston Churchill in full flow in the USA in 1950. Four years earlier on a speaking tour of America, in March 1946, he had warned of the dangers that faced post-war Europe as 'police governments' took over in Eastern Europe: 'This is certainly not the liberated Europe we fought to build up. Nor is it the one which contains the essentials of permanent peace.'

had no intention of exchanging Nazi occupation for Soviet domination. In 1948 the Soviet Union broke off relations with Yugoslavia, which was expelled from the communist bloc.

By 1947 the US had fully woken up to the fact that the USSR was no longer a gallant wartime ally but a brutal dictatorship which trampled over any sign of opposition. George Kennan, a leading American foreign affairs expert, put forward the theory that Stalin's main aim was to ensure that the Soviet Union *'filled every nook and cranny available to it in the basin of world power.'* In response the United States adopted a policy of containing communism. This meant opposing the Soviet Union wherever possible.

The Yugoslav resistance leader Marshal Tito (far right) with his staff at their mountain headquarters in 1944. Tito was Yugoslavia's prime minister from 1945 to 1954 and then became President. He died in 1980. In all that time Yugoslavia was the only European communist country that refused to be part of the USSR's communist bloc.

Berlin children pose for the camera while a Dakota transport aircraft swoops over their vantage point to supply the blockaded city in the summer of 1948.

The Berlin Airlift

Berlin was cut off from the Western zones of Germany by over 160 km of the Soviet zone. Road and rail links to the two million inhabitants of West Berlin, and their electricity supply, were cut by the Soviets on 23 June 1948. At that point there was only enough food to last West Berliners a month and coal for 10 days. The Western powers decided to beat the blockade with a massive airlift. On 26 June the first US C-54 Skymaster transports landed at Gatow and Tempelhof airfields in Berlin. The city was now totally dependent on the air shuttle. Eventually 277,264 flights were made. The biggest lift was made on 16 April 1949 when 1,398 flights delivered nearly 13,000 tonnes, with an aircraft landing every minute. On 12 May 1949 the Soviets admitted defeat and lifted the blockade. Nevertheless, the lift continued until the end of September, by which time over 2.3 million tonnes had been flown into Berlin.

The new confrontation between the superpowers was felt most keenly in Berlin, the one hole left in the Iron Curtain. In East Berlin it was possible to buy a subway ticket to West Berlin and travel on to Western-occupied zones of Germany. Many East Berliners made the journey and never returned.

In March 1948 the British Foreign Secretary, Ernest Bevin, persuaded France, Belgium, Luxembourg and the Netherlands to join together to form a military alliance, the Western European Union. At the top of its agenda was the formation of a democratic West German government.

In protest the Soviet Union withdrew from the Allied Control Council, which oversaw the administration of occupied Germany. The USA, France and Britain then merged their zones into a single unit. Its economy was given an immediate boost by the introduction of the Deutschmark, a new currency. Within weeks industrial output had leaped ahead by 25 per cent and the shops began to fill with consumer goods.

The Soviets regarded this as the final straw. Their own zone of occupation was now facing a strong new West Germany, whose economic success might prove irresistibly attractive to the people in the East. The Soviet Union decided to blockade West Berlin, which was isolated deep inside the Soviet zone of occupation. The Western powers broke the blockade with a remarkable airlift (see box on page 34).

The Berlin airlift solidified the battle lines of the Cold War. In April 1949 the United States, Canada and ten Western European states formed a defensive alliance, the North Atlantic Treaty Organization (NATO). NATO's purpose was to deter a direct Soviet attack on Western Europe. West Germany joined NATO in 1954. The Soviet answer was the Warsaw Pact, signed in May 1955 by the Soviet Union, Albania, Bulgaria, Czechoslovakia, East Germany, Hungary, Poland and Romania.

Germany had been permanently divided in 1949. West Germany (the Federal Republic of Germany) came into being in September 1949, closely followed by East Germany (the German Democratic Republic). After 1949 the hostility between their governments worsened the tensions between the West and the Soviet Union. Germany became the symbol of the Cold War. However, the very fact that Germany was divided overcame the problem which had led to two World Wars - a powerful, populous and united Germany in central Europe. Not everyone rejoiced when the Berlin Wall came down in 1989.

Soviet tanks in Prague, Czechoslovakia, in 1968 reinforce the USSR's control after the government of Alexander Dubček had attempted to dismantle the harsher elements of communist rule.

Japan: A new sun rises

Fraternizing with the enemy: US soldiers make some Japanese friends in Yokohama in August 1945.

The Allied occupation of Japan began in the small hours of 28 August 1945 when the first group of US soldiers landed at an airfield near the city of Yokohama.

The Americans made their way into Yokohama through a wasteland of rubble and ruined houses in which thousands of Japanese lived in makeshift shelters. In the last six months of the war Japan's cities had been flattened by US bombers. Two of them, Hiroshima and Nagasaki, had been devastated by atomic bombs. Millions of people had fled into the countryside. Most were living on the edge of starvation.

Surrender on 15 August 1945 had dealt a shattering blow to Japan, which had previously never suffered military defeat. Now defeat was total. Victory in the Pacific war had been overwhelmingly achieved by the United States, and the Allied occupation which began in the summer of 1945 was almost completely US-run.

The man in charge of the occupation was General Douglas MacArthur, Supreme Commander Allied Powers (SCAP) and the architect of victory in the Pacific. President Truman gave MacArthur sweeping powers which enabled him to ignore the Allied Council set up to advise him. For five years from 1945 to 1950, MacArthur was the sole ruler of Japan.

From his headquarters in Tokyo, MacArthur began the 'demilitarization' of Japan. All remaining industry geared directly to the production of weapons was dismantled. Many of those who had been prominent in wartime organizations - including leading industrialists and senior military officers - were removed from their posts. Public funds were withdrawn from the Japanese

religion, Shinto, which was closely associated with the Japanese nationalism that had been one cause of the war in the Far East and Pacific. Banknotes were withdrawn if they bore 'undesirable' images such as Shinto symbols or the portraits of military leaders. Japanese newspapers were heavily censored. They were forbidden to mention the atomic bomb attacks on Hiroshima and Nagasaki in case they disturbed 'public tranquility'.

Makeshift huts in the ruins of Yokohama, the target of a series of devastating American bombing raids in the closing months of the war in the Far East.

MacArthur secured the co-operation of the Japanese people by insisting that their Emperor, Hirohito, remained on the throne. Any attempt to remove him would have provoked a fierce Japanese reaction. Hirohito was granted immunity from prosecution as a war criminal. In return he agreed to renounce his divinity. On 1 January 1946 the Emperor announced that he was no longer a god. To underline Hirohito's new image, he was photographed relaxing in his swimming pool. The Imperial princesses were shown washing up the dinner dishes in their summer villa.

General Douglas MacArthur reviews occupation troops in Japan on 4 July 1949. As Governor of Japan from 1945 to 1950 MacArthur enjoyed almost unlimited power. From July 1950 to April 1951 he served as Commander-in-Chief of the United Nations forces in the Korean War.

The Japanese Emperor Hirohito in 1949. After the war he renounced his divine role and became an important instrument of the US occupation of Japan. Here, instead of wearing traditional clothing he wears a Western-style frock coat.

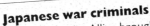

Japanese war criminals

In May 1946 the Allies brought 28 people accused of war crimes to trial in Tokyo. At the end of the 30-month trial seven were sentenced to death. Among them was General Hideki Tojo, who had been Japanese Prime Minister and War Minister from 1941 to 1944. Tojo had tried to commit suicide before his arrest. He mounted a dignified defence of his actions, and he showed no remorse. Tojo and six others were hanged in Sugamo prison on 23 December 1948. The US Army tried lesser war criminals in the city of Yokohama. Over 1,000 were tried, of whom 200 were acquitted, 124 sentenced to death and 62 to life imprisonment. In other locations in the Far East, Allied courts tried another 5,700 Japanese, convicting 4,405 and sentencing 984 to death. Some wartime atrocities committed by the Japanese were hushed up. Japanese scientists had conducted a series of horrific bacteriological experiments on live prisoners of war. The Japanese referred to their victims as 'logs of wood'. Instead of prosecuting the men who had carried out these experiments, the USA began working with them to develop new forms of biological warfare.

The Emperor was an important tool of MacArthur's demilitarization policy. The USA had devised the policy but they were careful to create the impression that it was being carried out by the Japanese themselves. The US aim was to reshape Japan along Western lines. In 1947 a new consititution was introduced. It provided for independent courts and judges, guarantees of political and civil liberty, and votes and equal property rights for women. When a Japanese minister attempted to delay the signing of the constitution, the flamboyant MacArthur waved a pistol in his face. The minister signed on the dotted line.

In Article 9 of the consititution Japan declared that it would forever renounce war and the threat of the use of force to settle international disputes. At first the USA had intended that Japanese trade and industry should operate only at a level sufficient to

At a converted war plant in 1947 Japanese women turn out clocks for export. From modest beginnings such as these grew the remarkable Japanese economic miracle of the 1950s.

keep the population employed and prevent the complete collapse of the economy. Later, realizing that this was impractical, the Americans introduced a number of economic reforms. A strong trade union movement was set up. Land reforms turned Japan's peasant farmers into landowners with a big stake in maintaining the new political and social system in Japan.

In the autumn of 1947 the occupation entered a new stage. The focus shifted from political and social reform to the rebuilding of the Japanese economy. Japan was to become the USA's most important ally in the western Pacific, where the Americans feared the spread of communist influence.

The USA could also sell its goods to Japan, but only if the Japanese economy prospered. US economic aid and advisers poured into Japan. As the ruined factories were rebuilt new technologies were introduced in every industry. The foundation was laid for the Japanese economic miracle of the 1950s.

Japan's return to wealth and favour was accelerated by events on the mainland of Asia. Japan's importance in the region was increased in December 1949, when the Chinese communists led by Mao Tse-tung defeated Chiang Kai-shek's Nationalist forces. The Nationalists withdrew to the island of Formosa (now Taiwan). The communists then controlled mainland China, where in October 1949 they had established a People's Republic.

Japanese women vote for the first time, in the post-war general election.

Crisis quickly followed in Korea. In August 1945 Soviet troops had overrun the Korean peninsula as far south as the 38th parallel - the limit of the occupation zone agreed between the USSR and the USA. This had become the frontier between two rival Korean republics: Chinese- and Soviet-backed in the north and US-supported in the south. When war broke out between the two states in June 1950, Japan became the all-important supply and staging base, repair centre and rest area for the US troops fighting in the war in Korea under the flag of the United Nations.

The Korean War, which lasted until July 1953, prompted the USA to change its opinion about Article 9 of the Japanese constitution (see page 38). Two weeks after the outbreak of the Korean War, MacArthur ordered the formation of a Japanese National Police Reserve of 75,000 men. It was to be equipped and trained by the USA as a 'Self Defence Force'. By the beginning of the 1990s Japan had the eighth-largest arms budget in the world. The USA's bitter enemy of the Second World War had become its most powerful ally in the Pacific.

Three players in the Korean War: a North Korean prisoner is brought in by a South Korean officer and an American soldier, Private Warren Benner, in July 1950. At the time of the Korean war, the USA's attitude to Japan changed. Japan went from being an occupied enemy to a Pacific outpost against communism.

Fragile peace

The Second World War bred a new sense of internationalism. Out of the ruins it was hoped that a new world would emerge. The mood was accurately caught by Sir William Beveridge, who had provided the blueprint for Britain's welfare state. He wrote, '. . . *the purpose of victory is to live in a better world than the old world.'*

The old world lay battered and bleeding. In Europe the immediate need for emergency aid was initially met by the United Nations Relief and Rehabilitation Administration (UNRRA). UNRRA had been set up in November 1943 to help the refugees of countries fighting Germany, Italy and Japan. The USA paid most of UNRRA'S bills, which were large. Its task involved caring for and resettling millions of refugees, and providing the raw materials and equipment for the rebuilding of agriculture, industry and communications.

UNRRA was one of the agencies of the United Nations Organization (UN), which came into being in June 1945. Its origins lay in the Atlantic Charter, signed by Roosevelt and Churchill in August 1941, which had spoken of a new 'system of general security'. During the war the Allies worked on plans for an international organization that would preserve the co-operation that led to the defeat of Germany and Japan. In the closing weeks of the war every nation which had declared war on Germany before 1 March 1945 was invited to a conference in San Francisco to prepare a Charter for the United Nations.

Birth of Israel: Israeli troops snatch a moment of rest during the battle for Jerusalem in October 1948. Britain, the old imperial power, had been in charge of Palestine, from which Israel was formed. In the next ten years most British colonies became independent.

Article 1 of the UN Charter listed the UN's aims as the safeguarding of world peace, protecting human rights, ensuring equal rights for all peoples and improving living standards throughout the world. The Charter also provided that all member states of the UN should be represented in a General Assembly. The most important part of the UN was the Security Council, consisting of 11 members, of whom six were elected for two-year terms by the General Assembly. The other five - the United States, Britain, the Soviet Union, France and China - were permanent members and had the right to veto any action proposed by the Security Council. The veto meant that the Security Council soon became a Cold War battleground between the USA and the USSR, each of which could block any action they disliked. The use of the veto became commonplace as the two adversaries glowered at each other across the table.

There was to be no Third World War, but neither was there to be peace after 1945. Greece had suffered cruelly from famine and German occupation. Now it was ravaged by a civil war between communists and supporters of the restored Greek monarchy. The communists were supported by Bulgarians, Albanians and Yugoslavs. Behind them stood the USSR. After the war the British had taken the responsibility of providing the Greeks with economic and military aid. The task proved beyond them, and the USA stepped in. The tide turned against the communists but the fighting lasted until October 1949.

A mule train supporting the Greek government against communist guerrillas moves up to the front line in the mountains in June 1947.

The British could no longer meet all their overseas commitments. They were overstretched in the Middle East. Under a United Nations mandate they were responsible for governing Palestine, the territory now known as Israel and seen by Jews throughout the world as their homeland. During the Second World War Jewish immigration to Palestine had been restricted. After the war many Jewish survivors of Nazi persecution wanted to resettle in Palestine. This was fiercely opposed by the Arab population there.

In 1947 the UN General Assembly voted to partition Israel into separate Arab and Jewish states. Violence between Arabs and Jews mounted. At the beginning of May 1948 the British pulled out. On 14 May the independent Jewish state of Israel was proclaimed. The next day Israel was invaded by the Arab states of Egypt, Iraq, Lebanon, Jordan and Syria. The state of Israel was born in bitter fighting which lasted until January 1949.

By the time the Korean War broke out in June 1950, the threat of atomic warfare had grown. Soviet scientists had exploded their first atom bombs in 1949, although the USA was to keep its lead in the nuclear race for many years to come. The USA believed that the key factor in bringing an end to the fighting in Korea - which cost over two million Korean lives - was their threat to use nuclear weapons against China, North Korea's ally. By then new and even more terrible bombs had been developed. In 1952 the Americans successfully tested a hydrogen bomb hundreds of times more powerful than the atomic bombs that had been dropped on Hiroshima and Nagasaki.

In Asia the European colonial powers - Britain, France and the Netherlands - were in retreat. At the end of the war 800 million people remained under their rule. But the defeats they had suffered at the hands of the Japanese in the first six months of the war had fatally damaged European prestige and encouraged Asian nationalists who wanted independence for their countries.

In 1947 the division of the British Indian Empire into the Hindu state of India and the Muslim state of Pakistan led to widespread violence. The picture shows Muslim refugees seeking safety in an old fort in the Indian city of New Delhi.

French paratroops drop into Dien Bien Phu in northeast Indochina in the spring of 1954. They were about to be defeated by communist forces under General Giap. Eventually the French withdrew from Indochina. Western dominance in the Far East was coming to an end.

The replacement of colonial by Japanese rule was a harsh experience for the nationalists, but they had also benefited in important ways. Resistance movements against the Japanese had been armed and trained from outside by the Allies. At the end of the war the nationalists had the weapons and organization to resist the returning colonial powers.

In the Far East the British fought a bitter and costly war to win back from the Japanese territories which they had already pledged to give away. Burma gained its independence in 1948. In 1947 India - the jewel in Britain's imperial crown - was partitioned into the two independent states of India and Pakistan. At the height of empire colonial possessions had been seen as a vital part of the economic strength of the European powers. Now they were a drain on European resources. Nevertheless, the Dutch and the French did not give up their colonies without a fight. In the Dutch East Indies four years of guerrilla war preceded the proclaiming of the Republic of Indonesia. In Indochina (now three countries: Vietnam, Cambodia and Laos) the French fought a long and costly war against communist forces. It ended in military defeat and French withdrawal in 1954. Vietnam was divided into two countries by the 17th Parallel. In the north there was a communist government backed by the USSR; in the south a regime supported by the USA. Ten years later the USA was drawn into a war in Vietnam that was to prove even longer and costlier than the first had for the French.

Glossary

Berlin Wall   A wall built in 1961 by the East German government, separating West Berlin from the rest of the city. It was built to try to stop the flow of refugees from East Berlin.

Charnel-house   A building in which the bones or bodies of the dead are stored.

Coalition government   A government made up of members of different political parties who agree to govern together.

Cold War   The political and economic war between the USA and its supporters on one side, and the USSR and its supporters on the other. The Cold War began soon after the Second World War and ended only in the early 1990s, with the collapse of the USSR.

Collaborator   Someone who works with people who have attacked his or her country. For instance, on the Channel Islands some government officials worked closely with the German Army, even though the Channel Islands were part of Britain. These officials have recently been accused of collaboration.

Communist bloc   The group of mostly Eastern European nations dominated by the USSR after the Second World War and during the Cold War.

Demobilization   The process of running down the armed forces after a war and returning the men and women called up in the conflict to civilian life.

Dunkirk   The evacuation of Allied troops from northern France in 1940, which avoided a terrible defeat.

Ethnic Germans   People who think themselves to be German, even though their homes could be outside the actual borders of Germany.

Final Solution   After a conference at Wansee in Berlin, during January 1942, Adolf Eichmann was put in charge of the 'Final Solution of the Jewish problem'. The solution was to get rid of all Jews, by herding them into death camps and killing them. This dreadful event is now often called the Holocaust.

Gestapo   Short for *Geheimstaatpolizei*, which means State Secret Police. The Gestapo had very wide powers throughout Germany and the occupied areas of Europe, and were one of the main Nazi organizations for terrorizing the people.

Hess, Rudolf   Hitler's deputy until September 1939. In May 1940 Hess flew alone to Britain on an unauthorized mission to try to make peace with England. In prison there he began to show signs of mental illness, which became worse during the Nuremberg trial. During the trial he was ignored by his co-defendants.

Lend Lease   The arrangement by which the USA supplied Britain

during the war.

Persecutor   Someone who ceaselessly tries to damage another person in some way.

Resistance   The underground groups in occupied Europe that fought a guerilla war against the Germans. The strength of the resistance varied from country to country. In France before the winter of 1943 the active members of the resistance numbered only a few thousand.

Ruhr   An industrial region in western Germany, which was heavily bombed by the Allies during the Second World War.

Scapegoat   A person who is blamed for an event even though he or she may not have been responsible for it. This could be done deliberately to shift the blame away from the person who is really responsible.

Show trial   A term often applied to the trials in the 1930s of former colleagues of the Soviet leader, Josef Stalin. False charges of treason were brought against them, untrue confessions were wrung from them, and their guilt was assumed by the press before the trials had even begun.

SS   Short for *Schutzstaffeln*, which means protection squads. The SS began as Hitler's personal bodyguard and became the most powerful Nazi organization. Commanded by Heinrich Himmler, it provided guards for the death camps and imposed Nazi rule throughout Europe. The *Waffen* (armed) SS fought alongside units of the regular German army.

Vichy   Vichy is a small town in France. When the Germans invaded France and occupied Paris, the country was split into two. One part was run by the Germans; the other was partly governed by the French, from the town of Vichy. After the war Vichy became another word for traitorous, although during the war many French people had gone along with the Vichy government.

Books to read

For older readers
Europe in Our Time Walter Laqueur (Viking, 1992)
Hour of the Women Christian von Krokow (Faber, 1993)
The Road Ahead Christabel Bielenberg (Bantam, 1992)
Where did the Forties Go? Andrew Davies (Pluto, 1984)

For younger readers
Britain Since1945 Nigel Smith (Wayland, 1990)
The United Nations Stewart Ross (Wayland, 1989)
The USA since 1945 Nigel Smith (Wayland, 1989)
The USSR under Stalin Stewart Ross (Wayland, 1991)

Contents

Introduction

A joyous greeting for an injured British serviceman on his return from the war. In the autumn of 1945 millions of servicemen and servicewomen were impatiently waiting to return to civilian life.

In the late summer of 1945 the world was exhausted by war. The cities of Germany and Japan had been levelled by Allied bombers. In Japan, Hiroshima and Nagasaki had been devastated by atomic bombs. In Germany things were no better. For every tonne of bombs the Germans had dropped on Britain during the war the British and Americans had dropped 315 tonnes on Germany.

Huge areas of Europe and Southeast Asia had been devastated by the fighting. Road, rail and canal systems had been destroyed. Ports were choked with wreckage. In Europe a severe drought followed by a disastrous harvest threatened famine in the worst-hit areas. In the parts of the Soviet Union that had been occupied by Germany the homes of six million families had been destroyed, leaving 25 million people homeless.

The human cost of the war had been horrific. The Poles had suffered worst of all. In Poland eight million people - one in four of the population - had died. The death toll in the Polish capital, Warsaw, was higher than the combined wartime casualties of Britain and the USA. In total as many as 55 million people may have died in the war.

Everywhere people were on the move. The derelict centre of Europe was filled with refugees - over ten million of them. Their ranks were swollen by deserters from various armies. Nineteen thousand deserters, the Lost Division, were Americans. By 1948 only 9,000 of these had been found. Other soldiers were coming home. The drawn-out process of demobilising the Allied forces was beginning, as millions of men and women stepped out of uniform and back into civilian life.

Where now? A trainload of refugees leaves eastern Germany for a new life in the west. Millions of ethnic Germans were driven out of the countries of eastern Europe at the end of the war. Those who travelled by train were the lucky ones: most were forced to walk halfway across Europe.

In the Far East some 4.5 million Japanese soldiers were disarmed and returned home within ten months of the Japanese surrender. They were joined by three million Japanese civilians who had colonized the empire Japan had won and then lost in Southeast Asia. Not so lucky were the 60,000 men of the Japanese Kwantung Army, which had surrendered to the Soviets in Manchuria in August 1945. They were sent to prison camps in Siberia. An equally grim fate awaited the millions of ethnic Germans forced out of the countries of Eastern Europe at the end of the war. In the winter of 1945 as many as two million of them died of exhaustion, disease and starvation on their march westward. Forcibly marched eastward at the same time were nearly six million Soviets who had been slave-labourers or prisoners of war, or who had deserted and fought for the Germans. When they arrived in the Soviet Union most of them were sent to labour camps.

In Europe the future looked bleak. The wartime alliance between the United States, Britain and the USSR was breaking up. Europe was being divided into two separate and hostile camps - one already dominated by the USSR, the other soon to be rescued from economic and political collapse by the USA. Yet within 15 years a remarkable economic recovery had been achieved. Germany and Japan, on their knees in 1945, had returned to their positions as dominant regional economic powers. But in 1960 the world remained divided between East and West, while growing nuclear arsenals and conventional forces threatened the peace won in 1945. It is only in the 1990s, with the collapse of the USSR and the end of the Cold War, that it can be said that the post-war era has come to an end.

A German woman weeps in the ruins of her home town. The heart of many European cities was nothing but rubble, and in the centre of Berlin people lived in the basements of bomb-damaged buildings with no heat or running water.

Crime and punishment

Churchill, Truman and Stalin at the Potsdam conference, where it was agreed that war criminals would be put on trial. Attitudes to the trial varied: Stalin was heard to say that 'The grand criminals should be tried before being shot.' In the end three of twenty-two defendants at the Nuremberg trials were freed, and twelve were sentenced to death.

As the war in Europe drew to a close, the Allies faced the problem of how to deal with the men who had inflicted such destruction and suffering on the continent. The Nazis had not stopped at the military defeat of enemies. They had gone on to enslave many of them. Sometimes they had killed whole populations. It was unthinkable that the leading Nazis should go unpunished for the crimes they had committed.

At first the Allies disagreed about the form the punishment should take. The British wanted to shoot the Nazi leaders as soon as they were captured. But the US President, Harry S Truman, insisted on a proper trial, to show the world the terrible truth about the Nazis and to restore confidence in the notion of justice. The Soviet Union agreed with Truman.

In July 1945, Germany had surrendered. Allied soldiers had entered the Nazi death camps, freeing the skeleton-like survivors and uncovering evidence of

how millions were murdered. The trial of 22 major war criminals opened on 20 November 1945 in the city of Nuremberg. It was here in the 1930s that the Nazis had staged their Party rallies. And it was at one of these rallies, in 1935, that Hitler had announced the so-called Nuremberg laws which made Jews second-class citizens in Germany - the first step towards the Final Solution.

The defendants at Nuremberg represented the German armed forces, government and Nazi Party. The most important Nazis of all were not in the dock. Adolf Hitler had committed suicide, as had his propaganda chief Dr Josef Goebbels and the head of the SS, Heinrich Himmler. Hitler's secretary and power-broker, Martin Bormann, had disappeared in the ruins of Berlin.

Defendants in the dock at Nuremberg. Hermann Goering sits with his chin in his hand on the far left. Next to him is slumped Rudolf Hess, who was ignored by his co-defendants throughout the trial. On Hess's left are Ribbentrop, formerly German foreign minister, and Keitel, chief of staff of the German army.

Their prosecutors and judges were drawn from the USA, USSR, Britain and France. The biggest of these was the USA, and the Americans dominated the trial at Nuremberg. The US legal team numbered 1,700. There were only 170 working for the British, and fewer for the French and Soviet teams.

The men in the dock at Nuremberg were charged with entering into a conspiracy with Hitler to commit crimes against peace and humanity, and war crimes. The British and US teams concentrated on the crimes against peace. The French and the Soviets handled the crimes against humanity. When it came to crimes against humanity, there was no shortage of evidence. The Germans had kept very careful records of the extermination of the Jews and other acts of barbarism.

One of the defendants at Nuremberg, Hans Frank, the Nazi governor-genral of Poland, said that *'a thousand years shall pass and the guilt of Germany will not be erased.'* Others were unrepentant. Hermann Goering, for many years the second most important man in Germany, defended himself vigorously. Most of the defendants, however, claimed that they were only obeying orders. One exception was Rudolf Hess, Hitler's former deputy, who sat through the trial in a daze, seemingly lost in a world of his own.

The judges delivered their findings on 30 September 1946 and the sentences on the following day. Twelve of the defendants (including the absent Martin Bormann) were sentenced to be hanged in the Nuremberg prison gymnasium on 16 October.

Three of the defendants were acquitted, although they were later tried on lesser charges and imprisoned. The rest received prison sentences of varying lengths, which they served in Berlin's Spandau prison. From 1966 Rudolf Hess, who had been sentenced to life imprisonment, was Spandau's only prisoner. He died there in 1987, aged 91.

Doubts have been expressed about the legality of the Nuremberg trial. The defendants were accused of violating international law, which applied to states and not individuals. The USSR had committed a war crime in 1939 when it invaded Finland, but this was swept under the carpet at Nuremberg. When the court was considering the German invasion of Poland in the same year, the lawyers were forbidden to refer to the secret agreement by which Poland was divided into two by Germany and the USSR. In their list of charges the French did not mention the 83,000 Jews sent to their deaths by the French government at Vichy during the German occupation of France.

It was important that the trials at Nuremberg should deter further wars of aggression and underline the determination of the newly formed United Nations Organization (UNO) to act decisively in the cause of peace and international justice. It was hoped that the Nuremberg trial would provide the basis for bringing future war criminals to justice. This has not happened. Today there

Hermann Goering

Goering cheated the hangman by swallowing a concealed cyanide capsule the night before his execution. It has been suggested that he obtained the capsule from one of his US guards in return for gifts which included a gold cigarette case, although the suicide note Goering left suggested this was not so. Goering's body, and those of the other executed Nazis, is said to have been burned in the ovens of the concentration camp at Dachau and then scattered in the Isar river.

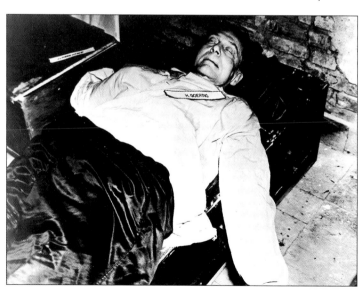

Hermann Goering lies dead after committing suicide by swallowing a cyanide capsule on the eve of his hanging.

are no means by which the principles established at Nuremberg can be enforced. Crimes against humanity are regularly committed today - as can be seen in the vicious civil war in the former Yugoslavia and the Iraqi dictator Saddam Hussein's persecution of the Kurdish people in northern Iraq. But there is little likelihood of a present-day Nuremberg trial to punish the war criminals of the 1990s.

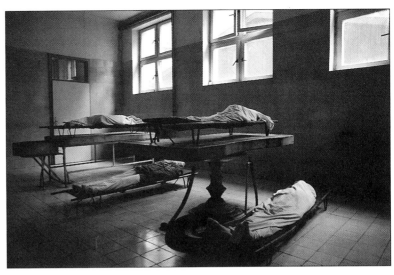

A children's hospital ward in Sarajevo, Bosnia. Although the United Nations had hoped that the Nuremberg trials would be the basis for deterring war crimes, this has not happened, even in Bosnia, where terrible war crimes have been committed.

Airey Neave was one of the British team at the Nuremberg Trial. Later he wrote: *'At the entrance to the Palace of Justice, a tram stopped beside us as we showed our passes. A row of hostile faces watched me. I stared back in anger. I was not yet ready to forgive or forget. The clothes of the passengers had the same drab colour as if they had risen from the tomb. Their expressions were fixed in misery and hate. The women especially looked at me with real bitterness. There was nothing to buy in the shops of Nuremberg. One could not buy a new hat, a new kettle, a yard of ribbon, a baby's napkin. They wore no makeup and their shoes let in the autumn rain. They bought the barest rations in the shops and took them to their wretched bombed-out homes where there was neither warmth or light. But I could feel no pity at this time as I confronted them. "It was Hitler who did this to you!" I shouted at them in German. They turned their faces from me.'*

The defendants at Nuremberg

EXECUTED: *Hans Frank*, governor of Poland; *Wilhelm Frick*, Interior Minister then governor of Bohemia-Moravia; *Hermann Goering*, Luftwaffe commander; *Dr Ernst Kaltenbrunner*, head of the SD (secret police); *Wilhelm Keitel*, chief of staff of German armed forces; *Alfred Jodl*, Keitel's deputy; *Joachim von Ribbentrop*, Foreign Minister; *Alfred Rosenberg*, Minister for Occupied Eastern Territories; *Fritz Sauckel*, head of slave labour programme; Arthur Seyss-Inquart, governor of the Netherlands; *Julius Streicher*, owner of the anti-Jewish newspaper Der Sturmer.

SENTENCED TO IMPRISONMENT: *Karl Dönitz*, Navy chief and Hitler's successor - 10 years; *Walter Funk*, President of Reichsbank - life; *Rudolf Hess* - life; *Konstantin von Neurath*, governor of Bohemia-Moravia to 1941 - 15 years; *Erich Raeder*, navy commander to 1943 - life, later commuted to 10 years; *Baldur von Schirach*, Hitler Youth leader and Gauleiter of Vienna - 20 years; *Albert Speer*, Armaments Minister - 20 years.

ACQUITTED: *Hans Fritzsche*, radio propaganda chief; *Franz von Papen*, chancellor in 1932, vice-chancellor in Hitler's first government; *Hjalmar Schacht*, Economics Minister in the 1930s.

Denazification

At the end of the war in Europe US troops in Germany received a stern warning from the US forces' newspaper Stars and Stripes: *'Don't Get Chummy With Jerry. . . In Heart, Body and Spirit Every German is Hitler.'* They were forbidden any contact with Germans outside their military duties. The punishment for fraternization - making friends with Germans - was a fine of $65, a month's pay. British soldiers who fraternized with the enemy faced similar fines and loss of rank.

Germany had been occupied as a defeated enemy nation and the Allies set about wiping out the Nazi past. The process was called Denazification. Many trials followed the proceedings at Nuremberg. German generals were charged with committing war crimes. Those in charge of planning and carrying out the Final Solution - the extermination of the Jews - were also brought to trial. Industrialists who ran their factories using slave labour were also tried.

August Hoehm, the second-in-command of the Sachsenhausen concentration camp, is cross-examined during a war crimes trial held in the Soviet sector of Berlin in the autumn of 1947. Although the Nuremberg trials were where the most famous Nazis were tried, many other trials were held.

One of the industrialists brought before a war crimes court was Alfred Krupp, who in 1942 succeeded his father as the head of the Nazis' largest arms organization. The Allies had wanted to try Krupp's father at Nuremberg, but decided that the old man was too ill to face trial, so they tried his son instead. In 1948 a court sentenced Alfred Krupp to 12 years in prison, and ordered the confiscation of all his property.

Timeline

1929   **October 29th** Wall Street Crash, triggers Great Depression.
1931   **April 14th** Spain becomes a republic.
1933   **January 30th** Hitler appointed Chancellor of Germany. **August 2nd** Hitler becomes Fuhrer (German dictator).
1935   **October 2nd** Italian troops invade Ethiopia.
1936   **February** Popular Front wins elections in Spain.
March 8th German troops enter Rhineland.
July 18th Rebellion by Army officers begins Spanish civil war. **November 1st** Italy and Germany sign Rome-Berlin Axis. **1937 July 7th** Japan attacks China. **November 6th** Italy, Germany and Japan sign the Anti-Comintern Pact.
1938   **March 12th** Anschluss (union of Germany and Austria) declared: German troops occupy Austria.
August-September International confrontation over Hitler's demands for part of Czechoslovakia (the Sudentenland).
September 30th Munich Conference resolves Czech crisis.
October 12th German troops occupy Sudetenland.

1939 **March 12th** German forces occupy Czechoslovakia. **28th** Franco's forces capture Madrid: Spanish civil war ends. **31st** France and Britain guarantee Polish independence.
May 2nd Germany and Italy agree Pact of Steel alliance. **August 23rd** USSR-German non-aggression pact agreed. **September 1st** Germany invades western Poland. **3rd** France and Britain declare war on Germany. **17th** Soviet troops invade eastern Poland.

1940 **April 7th** Norway and Denmark attacked by Germany. **May 10th** German troops begin invasion of Netherlands, Belgium and Luxembourg. Churchill becomes British prime minister. **12th** Germany begins invasion of France.
June 10th Italy declares war on Britain and France.
14th German forces capture Paris. **22nd** French sign armistice at Compiegne. Battle of Britain begins.
September 27th Germany, Italy and Japan sign the Tripartite Pact. **November 5th** Roosevelt re-elected US president. **14th** Coventry, England, levelled by German bombers.

1941 **March 11th** Lend-Lease Act signed. **April 17th** Germany starts invasion of Balkans and Greece. **June 22nd** Invasion of USSR by Germany (Operation Barbarossa) begins.
July US oil embargoes on oil and steel exports to Japan. **August 14th** Roosevelt and Churchill sign Atlantic Charter, agreeing war aims. **November** German forces halted outside Moscow.

December 7th Japan bombs US naval base at Pearl Harbor, Hawaii. Japan declares war on USA. **8th** USA and Britain declare war on Japan. **11th** Germany and Italy declare war on USA: USA declares war on them.

1942 **February 15th** Singapore captured by Japanese. **April 9th** US forces on Bataan Peninsula surrender. **May 6th** US forces on Corregidor surrender. **July** Battle of Stalingrad begins.
November 8th US and British troops land in North Africa. **11th** German forces enter Vichy France.

1943 **January 14-24th** Casablanca Conference agrees Allied war aim of unconditional enemy surrender. **February 2nd** German army at Stalingrad surrenders. **May 12th** War ends in North Africa. **July 10th** Allied forces land in Sicily.
26th Mussolini resigns. **September 3rd** Allies land in Italy. **8th** Italy surrenders. **10th** Nazi forces occupy Rome. **November 22-25th** Cairo Conference.
28th Tehran Conference opens.

1944 **March** Soviet troops enter Poland.
June 4th Allied troops enter Rome.
6th D-day: Allied invasion of France begins. **July 20th** Hitler wounded in assassination attempt by German officers. **21st** Dumbarton Oaks conference lays down basis for United Nations. **August** Warsaw Uprising starts. **25th** Paris liberated. **October** Warsaw Uprising crushed. **6th** Soviet forces enter Hungary and Czechoslovakia. **20th** US forces enter Philippines.
November All-out US bombing of Japan begins.
December 16th German troops attack through Ardennes.

1945 **February 4th** Yalta conference.
April 1st US forces occupy Okinawa.
12th Roosevelt dies: Truman US president. **20th** Soviet forces enter Berlin. **28th** Mussolini executed. **May 1st** Hitler's suicide announced in Berlin. **2nd** Berlin captured. **7th** Germany signs unconditional surrender.
June 26th UN formed. **July 17th** Potsdam conference opens. **August 6th** Atomic bomb dropped on Hiroshima. **8th** Atomic bomb dropped on Nagasaki.
September 2nd Japan signs surrender.

1946   **March 5th** Churchill's 'Iron Curtain' speech.
1947   **March 12th** Truman Doctrine outlined.
June 5th Marshall Plan put forward.
1948   **June 24th** USSR begins blockade of West Berlin (ends May12th 1949).

Index

Bold numbers refer to text accompanied by a picture.